WELCOME TO

THE GIGANTIC GEOGRAPHY QUIZ BOOK

Lunar Press is a privately-run publishing company which cares greatly about the accuracy of its content.

As many questions in this quiz book are subject to change, please email us at lunarpresspublishers@gmail.com if you notice any inaccuracies to help us keep our questions as up-to-date as possible.

Happy Quizzing!

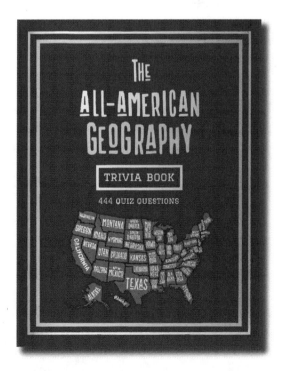

CONTENTS

Answers

EUROPE

1. Which European country is famous for its boot-shaped peninsula?

2. Spain is geographically separated from continental Europe by which mountain range?

3. The Volga is Europes longest river. How many kilometres long is it?
a. 1,820   b. 2,640   c. 3,690   d. 4,380

4. Hungary is bordered by seven countries; Slovakia, Ukraine, Romania, Serbia, Croatia, and Slovenia. What is the seventh country?
a. Austria   b. Poland   c. Bulgaria   d. Bosnia and Herzegovina

5. How many federal states is Germany divided into?
a. 4   b. 8   c. 12   d. 16

6. What are the three Baltic countries?

7. What is the capital of Slovakia?
a. Belgrade   b. Chisinau   c. Minsk   d. Bratislava

8. The tallest mountain in Europe is Mount Elbrus, how many meters tall is it?
a. 5,284   b. 5,642   c. 5,994   d. 6,209

9. Which country in Europe has the highest life expectancy with 83.1 years?
a. Greece   b. Germany   c. France   d. Spain

10. It is often debated whether Mount Elbrus should be considered as being in Europe. What is the tallest mountain in the Alps, which is often considered the tallest in Europe?

11. Besides the Iberian Peninsula, what are the other two great peninsulas of southern Europe?

12. Europe has 82 volcanoes, how many of these are located in Iceland?
a. 8   b. 15   c. 24   d. 32

13. The Madeira Islands belong to which country?
a. Spain   b. Italy   c. Portugal   d. Greece

14. Jersey is one of the Channel Islands that form an archipelago in the English Channel. How many of the three other Channel Islands can you name?

15. Gdańsk is located in which country?
a. Poland   b. Ukraine   c. Russia   d. Hungary

16. What name is Ireland often referred to as, due to its green rolling hills?

17. In which European city is Disneyland located?

18. Which two countries occupy the Iberian Peninsula?

19. Which of the following is the nickname of Toulouse in France?
a. The Blue City   b. The Green City   c. The Pink City

20. Edinburgh is the capital of Scotland but what is the largest city in Scotland by population?
a. Aberdeen   b. Dundee   c. Paisley   d. Glasgow

21. What is mainland Europe's northernmost capital city?
a. Oslo   b. Helsinki   c. Stockholm   d. Brussels

22. How many countries does Switzerland share a border with?
a. 3   b. 4   c. 5   d. 6

23. Russia is the largest country in Europe by population, but which country is the smallest?

24. The Rhine Falls is the largest plain waterfall in Europe. In which country are the falls located?
a. Austria   b. Switzerland   c. Germany   d. France

25. Which country has the longest coastline in Europe?
a. Greece   b. United Kingdom   c. Italy   d. Norway

26. Lake Annecy is located in which country?

27. What is Europes largest lake?
a. Lake Onega, Russia   b. Lake Vänern, Sweden
c. Lake Ladoga, Russia   d. Lake Saimaa, Finland

28. What is the name of the famous church located in Barcelona, Spain, where construction started in 1882?

29. Salisbury Plain in Wiltshire, UK, is home to which famous prehistoric monument?

30. How many countries does Europe consist of?
a. 44   b. 49   c. 53   d. 57

31. What is the name of the river that flows through Rome?

32. Istanbul is the most populous city in Europe, but what is the most densely populated country?
a. Malta   b. San Marino   c. Netherlands   d. Monaco

33. The Eiffel Tower is visited by millions each year, making it the most visited monument that you have to pay for in the world. Just how many people visit each year?
a. 4 million   b. 7 million   c. 11 million   d. 15 million

34. Europe is home to the world's largest Church. In which country can you find it?

35. Which country is the most sparsely populated in Europe?
a. Iceland   b. Norway   c. Sweden   d. Finland

36. Europe has 16 landlocked countries. Which is the largest landlocked country?
a. Serbia   b. Czechia   c. Belarus   d. Poland

37. Which sea is found between Greece and Turkey?
a. Caspian Sea   b. Black Sea   c. Aegean Sea   d. North Sea

38. The Alps mountain range is the highest and longest mountain range in Europe. How many Alpine countries does it cross?
a. 2   b. 4   c. 6   d. 8

39. What is the name of Norway's most famous fjord?

40. Which country in Europe has the most UNESCO World Heritage Sites?
a. Germany   b. Norway   c. Italy   d. United Kingdom

41. What is the biggest island in Europe?

42. What is the southernmost capital of Europe?
a. Lisbon   b. Valletta   c. Athens   d. Tirana

43. This hilltop temple monument is Greece's number one tourist attraction. What is it called?

44. The Azores are an archipelago composed of nine volcanic islands. What country are they part of?
a. Portugal   b. Spain   c. Greece   d. Montenegro

45. What is the capital of Norway?

46. Which sea separates Europe and Africa?

47. The Danube river runs 1,780 miles. Where does the river begin and end?

48. Andorra, Luxembourg, and Monaco are all countries that share a name with their capitals. Name two other countries in Europe that also share a name with their capitals.

49. In which country can the mountain Sierra Morena be found?
a. Italy   b. France   c. Austria   d. Spain

50. Which is the second largest country in Europe by area?

51. Europe is made up of many peninsulas. What is the largest peninsula in Europe?
a. Iberian   b. Balkan   c. Italian   d. Scandinavian

52. Which country in Europe has the largest port?

53. How many countries border the Czech Republic?
a. 1   b. 3   c. 4   d. 6

54. What is the capital city of Hungary?

55. This country is known for its forests, lakes and popular shop IKEA. Which country is it?

56. Norway has the second most islands in Europe. Which country has the most islands in Europe with 221,831?

57. Finland has the most lakes in Europe. How many lakes does it have?
a. 45,000   b. 120,000   c. 188,000   d. 210,000

58. When did the Netherlands officially drop their support of the word Holland?
a. 2014   b. 2016   c. 2018   d. 2020

59. Where are the Spanish Steps located?

60. What are the two countries that border directly north of Hungary?
a. Czechia   b. Austria   c. Croatia   d. Serbia   e. Slovakia

ASIA

1. Mt. Fuji is the highest mountain in which country?

2. What is the longest river in Asia?
a. Mekong River   b. Yangtze River   c. Yellow River   d. Ob River

3. The Euphrates is Western Asia's longest river. How many kilometres does it run?
a. 2245   b. 2760   c. 3490   d. 3981

4. Which two countries is the tiny country of Bhutan sandwiched between?

5. The Himalayan mountain range crosses five countries. Bhutan, India, and Nepal are three of the five, what are the final two countries?

6. What is the highest mountain in Asia called?

7. What is the name of the strait that separates Korea from Japan?
a. Tsushima Strait   b. Malacca Strait   c. Sunda Strait

8. Which US state is slightly larger than Iran?

9. As of 2023, what percentage of the world live in China and India?
a. 24%   b. 30%   c. 36%   d. 42%

10. Asia's largest desert, covers roughly 1,300,000 square kilometres across southern Mongolia and northern China. What is the name of this desert?

11. China and India are separated by a mountain range. What is the name of this famous mountain range?

12. Which country in Asia has the most islands?
a. Philippines   b. Malaysia   c. Japan   d. Indonesia

13. In which country is Angkor Wat located?
a. Laos   b. Cambodia   c. Vietnam   d. Thailand

14. What is the capital city of the Philippines?

15. Also known as a sea, what is the largest lake in Asia?

16. Asia has 491 active volcanoes. Which country has the most volcanos?
a. Indonesia   b. Japan   c. Philippines   d. China

17. The Mayon Volcano is located in which country?

18. The Ganges River is a sacred body of water to the Hindus. Which two countries does the river flow through?

19. In which country would you find the city of Phuket?

20. What is the largest city in Pakistan?

21. How many countries are there in Asia?
a. 33   b. 41   c. 48   d. 56

22. South Asia and Southeastern Asia are two regions of Asia. How many regions does Asia have in total?
a. 2   b. 4   c. 5   d. 7

23. How many countries does China border?
a. 6   b. 8   c. 11   d. 14

24. Which country has the lowest population density in Asia?
a. Mongolia   b. Oman   c. Kazakhstan   d. Laos

25. How many countries in Asia are landlocked?
a. 4   b. 7   c. 10   d. 12

26. In 2022, China was the most visited country in Asia. What was the second most visited country?

27. One of the 7 wonders of the world can be found in India. What is it?

28. Asia is the largest of the world's continents. What percentage of the Earth's land area does it cover?
a. 20%   b. 30%   c. 40%   d. 50%

29. True or false: the Himalayas is shrinking by approximately 1cm per year.

30. Which country has the largest urban area in Asia?

31. Asia is the most populous continent. What was the total population of Asia in 2022?
a. 2.7 billion   b. 3.7 billion   c. 4.7 billion   d. 5.7 billion

32. Where can Jeju Island be found?

33. The largest species of monitor lizards can be found on which island in Indonesia?

34. One of the seven natural wonders of the world is located in Vietnam. What is it called?

35. Maldives consists of 1190 coral islands, with the largest being its capital with 92,500 inhabitants. What is the name of this island?

36. There are five countries which have land in both Europe and Asia. Name three of these countries.

37. Borneo is the third largest island in the world. Which three countries does it belong to?

38. South East Asia is home to the world's largest flower, which is known as the corpse flower due to its bad smell. What is the name of this flower?
a. Corypha umbraculifera   b. Neptune Grass   c. Rafflesia arnoldii

39. What is the capital of Vietnam?

40. One sea in Asia has the lowest elevation and lowest body of water on the surface of Earth. Which sea is this?

NORTH AMERICA

1. Which city is the largest in North America by population?
a. New York City   b. Mexico City   c. Los Angeles   d. Chicago

2. Which state in the US is the most populated?
a. Texas   b. Florida   c. New York   d. California

3. The two longest rivers in North America are said to be within one kilometre of each other in length, at 3767 km and 3766 km respectively. What is the name of both of these rivers?

4. North America is home to the hottest place on earth. What is it called?

5. The highest mountain in North America has a summit elevation of 6,190 metres (20,310 feet) above sea level. What is the name of this mountain?

6. Lake Huron is the second largest lake in North America by area. What is the largest lake?

7. How many islands make up the Caribbean?
a. 200   b. 300   c. 500   d. 700

8. Which island is the biggest in the Caribbean?
a. Marie-Galante   b. Hispaniola   c. Grand Cayman   d. Acklins

9. What is the name of the huge sculpture of four presidents in the US?

10. What is the name of the fifth longest river in North America, which makes up a 2020 km segment of the border between the United States and Mexico?

11. Which country is the largest in North America by area?

12. How many countries does North America consist of?
a. 8   b. 12   c. 18   d. 23

13. The smallest country in North America is Saint Kitts and Nevis.
What is the population of this country?
a. 18,000   b. 54,000   c. 98,000   d. 158,000

14. The Continental Divide runs north and south of which mountain
range?

15. What is the name of the broad areas of flatland, which can be
found west of the Mississippi River and east of the Rocky Mountains,
which is predominantly covered in grassland and prairie?

16. How many provinces is Canada divided into?
a. 8   b. 10   c. 12   d. 14

17. North America is home to one of the most important waterways
in the world which connects the Atlantic and Pacific oceans. What is
its name?

18. Death Valley's Badwater Basin in Furnace Creek, California, is the
lowest elevation in North America. How many metres below sea level
is it?
a. 86   b. 115   c. 158   d. 191

19. What percentage of the North American population lives in the
US?
a. 57%   b. 64%   c. 69%   d. 75%

20. What percentage of Greenland is covered in ice?
a. 40%   b. 60%   c. 80%   d. 90%

21. What is the largest Canadian province by area?

22. Name the Canadian state with the highest population.

23. Which US state has the longest coastline at 106,000 km?
a. Florida   b. California   c. Hawaii   d. Alaska

24. The Hoover Dam was built in an effort to stop flooding. In what river is the Hoover Dam located?
a. Columbia River   b. Yukon River
c. Colorado River   d. Red River

25. North America is home to some of the youngest mountains on earth, with some peaks only beginning to form about a million years ago. What mountain range is it?
a. Alaska Range   b. Cascade Range
c. Sierra Nevada   d. Olympic Mountains

26. The Great Lakes are the largest freshwater system in the world. What are the names of the five lakes?

27. What percentage of the world's freshwater do the Great Lakes hold?
a. 8%   b. 12%   c. 17%   d. 20%

28. Which US state is the only one to be triply landlocked?
a. Ohio   b. Montana   c. Nebraska   d. Utah

29. What is the name of the tallest volcano in the US, which can be found in Hawaii?

30. Which Canadian city is the largest by population?
a. Montreal   b. Toronto   c. Vancouver   d. Calgary

31. North America has four major desert regions. Great Basin Desert and Sonoran Desert are two of the four major desert regions, what are the other regions called?

32. Which of the following states has the most national parks in the US with 9?
a. Alaska   b. Hawaii   c. California   d. Utah

33. North America borders four major bodies of water, three of which are oceans. Name two of the bodies of water.

34. True or false: North America is the only continent with every type of climate.

35. What colourful lights can be seen in the sky from Alaska?

36. What is the capital city of Canada?

37. The largest national park in Canada is so large that you could fit the entire country of Switzerland inside it, but what is it called?
a. Banff National Park   b. Fundy National Park Of Canada
c. Elk Island National Park   d. Wood Buffalo National Park

38. How many time zones is the United States divided into?
a. 3   b. 5   c. 6   d. 8

39. Name the Canadian province which is the only one to have French as its official language.

40. San Francisco is home to what famous suspension bridge?

41. Which US national park has some of the world's most active geysers, and has approximately 500 geysers in total?

42. Copper Canyon is located in which Mexican state?
a. Guerrero   b. Chihuahua   c. Morelos   d. Sinaloa

43. How many states is Mexico divided into?
a. 25   b. 31   c. 37   d. 43

44. The unofficial capital of the US, New York, is also known by which nickname?

45. What are the volcanic plugs in Saint Lucia called?
a. Pitons   b. Balons   c. Shairs   d. Doloms

46. North America is separated from Asia by which strait?

47. The world-famous Niagara Falls is located between which two lakes?
a. Crater Lake   b. Lake Powell   c. Lake Erie   d. Lake Ontario

48. Niagara Falls is made up of three waterfalls. The Horseshoe Falls and the American Falls are two, but what is the final waterfall?

49. What is the largest plateau located in North America?
a. The Mississippi Plateau   b. The Oregon Plateau
c. The Colorado Plateau   d. The Arizona Plateau

50. Silicon Valley is famous for its software and computer industry, but in which city would you find it?
a. Portland   b. San Francisco   c. Reno   d. Phoenix

51. The American Museum of Natural History, the biggest museum in the world, is located in North America, but in which city would you find it?

52. As of 2023, what is the population of Panama?
a. 1.8 million   b. 4.5 million   c. 7.8 million   d. 10.1 million

53. Arizona, Colorado, Utah and which other state meet at Four Corners Monument and Tribal Park?
a. Texas   b. Kansas   c. Nevada   d. New Mexico

54. Death Valley is the driest place in North America, but just how much rainfall do they get on average annually?
a. 2.2 cm   b. 5.6 cm   c. 11.4 cm   d. 18.1 cm

55. The longest river in Canada is 3,190 km long, but what is it called?

56. What is the capital of Cuba?

57. An imaginary line marks the northern line of the tropics and runs through North America. What is this imaginary line called?
a. Tropic of Cancer   b. Tropic of Capricorn

58. By area, which is larger: Greenland or Mexico?

59. What position does North America rank in when it comes to the population in relation to the other continents?
a. 2nd   b. 3rd   c. 4th   d. 5th

60. Where does the word America come from?

CENTRAL AMERICA

1. How many countries does Central America consist of?
a. 3   b. 5   c. 7   d. 10

2. Tajumulco is Central America's tallest volcano. In which country can it be found?
a. El Salvador   b. Guatemala   c. Nicaragua   d. Panama

3. What is the capital city of Belize?
a. Belmopan   b. Tegucigalpa   c. San Salvador   d. San José

4. Honduras is bordered by three countries, but which three are they?

5. The smallest country in Central America by population is approximately 10 times smaller than the second smallest country. Which country is the smallest?
a. El Salvador   b. Panama   c. Nicaragua   d. Belize

6. Approximately 28% of Costa Rica is national parks. How many national parks does Costa Rica have?
a. 7   b. 15   c. 28   d. 44

7. What is the total population of Central America as of 2023?
a. 185 million   b. 294 million   c. 408 million   d. 539 million

8. Caracol is a large ancient Maya archaeological site. In which country can this be found?
a. Guatemala   b. Panama   c. El Salvador   d. Belize

9. Which country is the white-faced capuchin monkey named after?

10. In which country would you find the ancient Maya city called Tikal?
a. Belize   b. Guatemala   c. Honduras   d. Nicaragua

11. What is the name of the lake that is the largest body of water in Central America?

12. The largest capital city of the region is Guatemala City. What was the population in 2022?
a. 1 million   b. 3 million   c. 5 million   d. 7 million

13. Name the southernmost country in Central America.
a. Panama   b. Nicaragua   c. El Salvador   d. Costa Rica

14. What is the official currency of El Salvador?

15. What is the capital city of Costa Rica?

SOUTH AMERICA

1. What is the highest waterfall in South America and also in the world?

2. Which mountain range is the longest in South America?

3. South America has two landlocked countries. Which of the following two countries are they?
a. Uruguay   b. Suriname   c. Ecuador   d. Bolivia   e. Paraguay

4. The Atacama Desert is the driest place in South America. In which country is this desert located?
a. Argentina   b. Chile   c. Peru   d. Bolivia

5. Off the coast of Bolívar Department in Colombia is the smallest island in South America. What is the island called?
a. Ilha Grande   b. San Andrés
c. Chiloé Island   d. Santa Cruz del Islote

6. How many countries does South America consist of?
a. 4   b. 7   c. 9   d. 12

7. Chile owns an island in the southeastern Pacific Ocean. What is the name of this island?
a. Salas y Gomez Island   b. Easter Island   c. Desventuradas Islands

8. Machu Picchu is an ancient royal city built by the Inca. In which country can it be found?

9. UNESCO World Heritage Site, The Galápagos Islands, are part of which country?

10. Patagonia is shared by which two countries?
a. Brazil   b. Argentina   c. Chile   d. Peru

11. What is the capital of Argentina?

12. In which country would you be if you were at the underground Salt Cathedral of Zipaquira?

13. The Amazon river is the longest in South America. How many kilometres does it run?
a. 4992   b. 5992   c. 6992   d. 7992

14. Which Empire flourished from 1200 - 1533 AD, starting in the Andean highlands of Peru.

15. In which country can you find the Torres del Paine National Park?
a. Argentina   b. Brazil   c. Chile   d. Paraguay

16. Which desert is considered the driest place in South America?

17. Which South American country is famous for its Carnival festival?

18. Which summit, located in Argentina, is the second highest of the world's Seven Summits after Mount Everest in Asia?

19. Bolivia and Peru both share the biggest lake. What is the name of this lake?

20. Which country is the largest country in South America by population?

21. What is the most populous city in South America?
a. Rio de Janeiro   b. Lima   c. Buenos Aires   d. São Paulo

22. In which country can the Christ the Redeemer statue be seen?

23. The Amazon rainforest is the largest tropical rainforest in the world. What percent of the rainforest can be found in Brazil?
a. 50%   b. 60%   c. 70%   d. 80%

24. Brazil is the highest-producing country for what?
a. Tea   b. Coffee   c. Rubber   d. Gun powder

25. South America is home to the world's largest salt flat. What is it called?

26. How many recorded languages does this continent have?
a. 45   b. 145   c. 450   d. 4,500

27. Which islands were the inspiration behind Darwin's theory of evolution?

28. What is the most southern point of South America?

29. How many miles long is the Atacama Desert in Chile?
a. 300   b. 600   c. 1100   d. 1,900

30. Name the three dependent territories which are part of South America.

31. Bolivia's capital is the highest in the world. What is the capital of Bolivia?

32. What is the smallest country in South America by population?
a. Guyana   b. Suriname   c. Paraguay   d. Bolivia

33. Bolivia is bordered by five countries. How many of these five countries can you name?

34. Brazil is comfortably the largest country in South America by population, but what is the population of Brazil as of 2023?
a. 115 million   b. 168 million   c. 213 million   d. 271 million

35. Which country is the second largest in South America, with a population of 51 million?

AFRICA

1. What is Africa's southernmost major city?

2. Up until 1919 Namibia was called a different name. What did Namibia use to be called?

3. Somalia has the longest national coastline in Africa. How long is the coastline?
a. 2222 km   b. 3333 km   c. 4444 km   d. 5555 km

4. Cape Town is home to which famous mountain?

5. Name the tallest mountain in Africa.

6. The Red Sea separates Africa from which other continent?
a. Europe   b. South America   c. Asia

7. The Democratic Republic of the Congo is Africa's second-largest country by area. What is the largest country in Africa?
a. Algeria   b. Libya   c. Sudan   d. Angola

8. The Zambezi River flows into which ocean?
a. Atlantic   b. Pacific   c. Indian   d. Arctic

9. Which country is home to the Zulu people?

10. Which African country has the nickname 'The Pearl of Africa'?
a. Chad   b. Liberia   c. Mali   d. Uganda

11. The Nile is the longest river in Africa. How many kilometres long is it?
a. 3845 km   b. 4610 km   c. 5708 km   d. 6650 km

12. The largest lake in Africa has a surface area of approximately 59,947 km. What is the name of this lake?
a. Lake Tanganyika   b. Lake Victoria   c. Lake Malawi

13. The most populated country in Africa has a population of about 206 million. Which country is this?
a. Egypt   b. DR Congo   c. Ethiopia   d. Nigeria

14. Africa is home to the largest desert in the world. What is the name of the desert?

15. This island is the largest island in Africa and the fourth largest in the world. What is it called?

16. South Africa is home to the largest green canyon in the world, what is it known as?

17. What is the second-highest mountain in Africa standing at 5199m?
a. Mount Stanley   b. Mount Speke
c. Ras Dashen   d. Mount Kenya

18. How many countries does Africa consist of?
a. 24   b. 34   c. 44   d. 54

19. The Great Pyramid at Giza can be found in which country?

20. What was Zimbabwe known as before the country's name was changed in 1980?

21. The fourth largest peninsula in the world is located in Africa. What is the name of this peninsula?
a. Cape Three Points   b. Turners Peninsula
c. The Horn of Africa   d. Cap-Vert

22. Which of the following is the smallest country in Africa by population?
a. Seychelles   b. Saint Helena
c. Sao Tome & Principe   d. Comoros

23. Mauritius was home to which extinct flightless bird, which could grow to heights of 1m?

24. What is the capital of Burkina Faso?
a. Antananarivo   b. Lusaka   c. Nouakchott   d. Ouagadougou

25. Which national park, located in Tanzania, is a UNESCO World Heritage Site, and is home to the largest lion population in Africa?

26. The Atlas Mountains start and end in which two countries?

27. Which country can the Masai Mara National Park be found in?
a. South Africa   b. Kenya   c. Ghana   d. Senegal

28. Which country is bordered by Libya, Sudan, the Central African Republic, Cameroon, Nigeria, and Niger?
a. Sudan   b. Tanzania   c. Chad   d. South Sudan

29. How many million inhabitants did Cape Town have in 2022?
a. 2.8 million   b. 3.8 million   c. 4.8 million   d. 5.8 million

30. What is Africa's national animal?
a. Lion   b. Elephant   c. Zebra   d. Springbuck

AUSTRALASIA

1. What is the capital of Australia?
a. Canberra   b. Sydney   c. Brisbane   d. Melbourne

2. How many islands does Tonga have?
a. 32   b. 169   c. 411   d. 994

3. The Great Barrier Reef is one of the most remarkable coral reefs in the world. Off which state in Australia can it be found?
a. Victoria   b. Queensland
c. South Australia   d. New South Wales

4. Lake Taupo is New Zealand's largest lake. What is the second-largest lake in New Zealand called?
a. Lake Wakatipu   b. Lake Wanaka   c. Lake Te Anau

5. What is New Zealand's longest river?
a. Rangitikei River   b. Whanganui River
c. Clutha River   d. Waikato River

6. The highest point in this country is on Kao Island, standing at 1,033 metres. In which country would you find this island?

7. In which country can the Varirata National Park be found?
a. Fiji   b. Vanuatu   c. Palau   d. Papua New Guinea

8. Which of the following is the largest lake in Australia?
a. Lake Torrens   b. Lake Eyre   c. Lake Frome   d. Lake Mackay

9. The highest mountain in Australasia is Mount Cook. Where can you find this mountain?

10. Kangaroos and koalas can only be found in which country?

11. What is the capital of New Zealand?

12. What is the name of the famous large sandstone rock that can be found in the southern part of the Northern Territory of Australia?

13. Samoa consists of two main islands. What are the names of these two islands?

14. Where can you find the world's largest raised coral atoll?
a. Tuvalu   b. Solomon Islands   c. Vanuatu   d. Australia

15. Which city in New Zealand has the nickname 'Garden City'?

16. The Blue Mountains can be found in which state in Australia?

17. Australia comfortably has the highest population in Australasia, but which country out of New Zealand and Papua New Guinea comes in second place?

18. How many islands belong to New Zealand?
a. 23   b. 210   c. 450   d. 600

19. The Māori name for New Zealand is Aotearoa. What does this translate to?
a. Lush green country   b. Long white cloud   c. Place of haven

20. Australasia is home to the world's largest natural harbour. In which city can this be found?

21. What is the capital city of Guam?
a. Hagåtña   b. Funafuti   c. Nuku'alofa   d. Palikir

22. Australia is known for its many animal and plant species. How many national parks does Australia have?
a. 416   b. 516   c. 616   d. 716

23. Which area in New Zealand gets the most rainfall, and is home to fjordlands and some of the most impressive waterfalls on the planet?

24. Port Moresby is the capital city of which country?

25. Tuvalu is an archipelago of how many islands?
a. 2   b. 9   c. 22   d. 98

ANTARCTICA

1. Antarctica is the highest continent in the world. What is its average elevation?
a. 1200 meters   b. 1800 meters   c. 2,500 meters   d. 3000 meters

2. What is the highest point in Antarctica?
a. Mount Faber   b. Mount Vinson   c. Mount Parade

3. Which three oceans touch Antarctica?

4. Does Antarctica have any volcanoes?

5. What animals are the only animals to breed on mainland Antarctica during the winter?

6. The largest glacier in the world is found in Antarctica. What is it called?
a. Thwaites Glacier   b. Pine Island Glacier
c. Denman Glacier   d. Lambert Glacier

7. A research base is located at the South Pole. What is the research base called?

8. What is the name of the Norwegian man who reached the South Pole first?
a. Robert Falcon Scott   b. Jules Dumont
c. Roald Amundsen   d. Sir Ernest Shackleton

9. Due to having little precipitation and vegetation, Antarctica is technically a what?

10. How many countries have territories in Antarctica?
a. 3   b. 7   c. 13   d. 20

11. What time zone does Antarctica use?
a. Greenwich Mean Time   b. Pacific Standard Time
c. Central Standard Time   d. Mountain Standard Time

12. Where can you walk through all 24 time zones in just seconds?

13. At the South Pole, in which months does the sun rise and set?
a. It rises in September and sets in March
b. It rises in March and sets in September

14. What is the coldest temperature ever recorded in Antarctica?
a. -58°C   b. -70°C   c. -89°C   d. -102°C

15. The Antarctic ice sheet is the largest on Earth, how many km does it cover?
a. 3 million km²   b. 8 million km²
c. 14 million km²   d. 22 million km²

RIVERS AND LAKES

1. Which lake is the lowest in the world at 427 metres below sea level?

2. Which of the following rivers flows through the Grand Canyon in Arizona?
a. Rio Grande   b. Colorado River   c. Yukon River   d. Red River

3. Which of the following is the longest river in Australia?
a. Murray River   b. Darling River   c. Murrumbidgee River

4. Which river carries the largest volume of water in the world, containing 20 percent of the Earth's fresh water?

5. Ullswater lake can be found in which country?
a. New Zealand   b. Ireland   c. Great Britain   d. Argentina

6. Lake Mckenzie is an incredible freshwater lake that only collects rainwater. On which island can you find Lake Mckenzie?
a. Tasmania   b. Fraser Island
c. Kangaroo Island   d. Philip Island

7. What is the longest river in Cambodia at 4350km long?

8. Nessie, a Scottish folklore creature, is said to be found in which lake in Scotland?

9. What is the beginning of a river called?

10. Lake Baikal is the deepest lake in the world. How deep is it?
a. 1,642 m   b. 2,301 m   c. 2,809 m   d. 3,221 m

11. Canada has the most lakes in the world. Which country has the second most lakes in the world?
a. Russia   b. United States   c. China   d. Brazil

12. Which country is the largest country without a lake or river, and is known as the "land of no rivers?
a. Saudi Arabia   b. Mauritius   c. Mali   d. Oman

13. The Roe River is recognized by the Guinness Book of World Records as the world's shortest river. How short actually is it?
a. 61 m   b. 98 m   c. 151 m   d. 227 m

14. Lake Huron is home to the largest island in any inland body of water in the world. What is the name of the island?

15. What do Lake Urmia, Lake Amadeus, Pink Lake, and Don Juan Pond all have in common?

16. What is the longest river in Canada, with a length of 4,241 km?

17. The River Seine can be found in which country?
a. Belgium   b. Netherlands   c. France   d. Denmark

18. The Colorado River system supplies how many people with drinking water?
a. 10 million   b. 25 million   c. 40 million   d. 55 million

19. What is the end of a river called?

20. What is the UK's longest river?
a. River Severn   b. River Trent   c. River Thames   d. River Tay

21. The Great Salt Lake is the largest saline lake in the US. In which state can this lake be found?
a. Louisiana   b. Missouri   c. Michigan   d. Utah

22. Which country has the nickname 'Land of the Thousand Lakes'?
a. Canada   b. Germany   c. Vietnam   d. Finland

23. How many million lakes are there on earth?
a. 3   b. 21   c. 56   d. 117

24. What are people who study inland waters called?

25. In 2007 a man swam the entire length of the Amazon river. What is the name of this man?

26. The Caño Cristales river in Columbia, known as the 'River of Five Colours', flows with bright blue, red, black, yellow, and green water. What causes the river to flow these varied colours?
a. Pollution   b. Aquatic plants   c. Elements in the rocks

27. What are subterranean rivers?

28. The Puerto Princesa Underground River flows underneath a mountain for five miles before emptying into the sea. In which country can this river bc found?
a. Tonga   b. Jamaica   c. Philippines   d. Cambodia

29. How long does the Caspian Sea stretch from north to south?
a. 800 km   b. 1200 km   c. 1600 km   d. 2000 km

30. The São Francisco River has a length of 2914 km, making it the fourth largest river in South America, but in which country would you find this river?

CAPITAL CITIES

1. What is the capital of Germany?

2. Ankara is the capital of which country?

3. Riga is the capital city of which country?

4. BKK is the airport code for which capital city?

5. I am visiting the capital of Kenya, what city am I in?

6. What is the capital city of North Korea?

7. Breaker Bay and Happy Valley are areas of which capital?

8. What is the capital of Jamaica?
a. Nassau   b. Kingston   c. Roseau   d. Havana

9. What capital city features in the 2001 film "Moulin Rouge"?

10. Vilnius is the capital of which European country?
a. Lithuania   b. Bulgaria   c. Albania   d. Romania

11. How many countries have capital cities with the same name as their country? An example of this is Mexico and Mexico City.
a. 8   b. 11   c. 14   d. 17

12. How many of these countries with capital cities with the same name as their country can you name?

13. Vientiane is the capital of which Asian country?
a. Sri Lanka   b. Cambodia   c. Indonesia   d. Laos

14. ATH is the airport code for which European capital?

15. Freetown is the capital city of which country?
a. Liberia   b. Sierra Leone   c. Senegal   d. Botswana

16. What is the largest capital city in Europe by population?
a. London   b. Moscow   c. Berlin   d. Istanbul

17. If I am in Colombo, which country am I in?

18. What is the capital city of Indonesia?

19. Which country is Managua the capital city of?
a. Belize   b. Micronesia   c. Nicaragua   d. Tuvalu

20. The Guinness Storehouse is located in which capital city?

21. What is the capital of Qatar?

22. The following is the capital city with the longest name: Krung Thep Mahanakhon Amon Rattanakosin Mahinthara Ayuthaya Mahadilok. This capital is known by a name which is far shorter and is the second most visited city per year. Which capital is it?

23. Seoul is the capital city of which country?

24. There is only one capital city which begins with the letter z. What is it?

25. If I am looking at La Sagrada Familia, what capital city am I in?

26. Tunis is the capital of what country?

27. If I am visiting the capital of Cambodia, which city am I in?
a. Hanoi   b. Phnom Penh   c. Ulaanbaatar   d. Funafuti

28. BEY is the airport code for which capital?

29. Which of the following cities has the highest population density in the world of all capital cities?
a. Singapore   b. Beijing   c. Dhaka   d. Manila

30. What is the capital city of Ecuador?

FLAGS

1. Which leaf is featured on the Canadian flag?

2. Which country has the oldest flag in the world?
a. Afghanistan   b. Turkey   c. Japan   d. Denmark

3. How many stars does the Australian flag feature?
a. 2   b. 4   c. 6   d. 8

4. What animal features on the Bhutan flag?

5. The flag for Ivory Coast can often be confused with which other country's flag?

6. How many flags are not rectangular?
a. 1   b. 3   c. 6   d. 10

7. What other country's flag does New Zealand's flag feature?

8. What is the United Kingdom's national flag called?

9. Which country's flag contains an image of the country?
a. Cyprus   b. Qatar   c. Belize   d. Albania

10. How many stars are on the Chinese flag?
a. 3   b. 5   c. 7   d. 10

11. What is the most common colour to feature on flags?
a. White   b. Red   c. Blue   d. Black

12. Which four of the following colours feature on the national flag of Mauritius?
a. White   b. Orange   c. Red   d. Yellow   e. Blue   f. Green

13. What shape does the Japanese flag feature?
a. Square   b. Circle   c. Triangle   d. Rectangle

14. What object is seen on the Liechtenstein flag?
a. Sword   b. Bear   c. Coins   d. Crown

15. The national flag of Italy is also known as what?

16. Which two of the following colours feature on the United Nations flag?
a. Blue   b. Purple   c. Orange   d. Black   e. Yellow   f. White

17. Which country's flag features an eagle with two heads?
a. Moldova   b. Madagascar   c. Wales   d. Albania

18. The Welsh flag has what mythical animal on it?

19. What countries flag can you find a golden lion holding a sword on?
a. India   b. Sri Lanka   c. Thailand   d. Mongolia

20. Which of the following countries flags features a green cedar tree?
a. Oman   b. Lebanon   c. Kuwait   d. Syria

21. The coat of arms of Mexico features an eagle eating what type of animal?
a. Mouse   b. Fish   c. Snake   d. Spider

22. What is the study of flags called?

23. Monaco and which other country have a virtually identical flag, with the upper half of the flag being red and the lower half being white?

24. The flag of which Southeast Asian country has a red background with a yellow star in the middle?

25. Which weapon can be found on the flag for Mozambique?
a. A cannon   b. An axe   c. A spear   d. An AK-47

26. Which is the only flag to have more than 4 sides?

27. What colours does the French flag feature?

28. Isreal features a symbol in the centre of its flag. What is the name of the symbol?

29. The Belize flag has the most unique colours, but how many different colours does it have?
a. 12   b. 17   c. 25   d. 33

30. How many times has the US flag been modified since 1777?
a. 3   b. 12   c. 19   d. 26

31. Which three colours are on the Italian flag?

32. Which of the following flags does not have a star on it?
a. Ghana   b. Syria   c. Cuba   d. Oman

33. Which country's flag has a plain blue background with a white star in the middle?
a. Madagascar   b. Somalia   c. Eswatini   d. Djibouti

34. The Irish flag is a vertical tricolour made up of green, white, and orange stripes. Which African flag is very similar to this, but just has the stripes in the opposite direction?
a. Mali   b. Côte d'Ivoire   c. Chad   d. Sudan

35. The flag of Austria contains which two colours?
a. Blue   b. White   c. Green   d. Black   e. Red

GUESS THE COUNTRY

1. This country is famous for Oktoberfest, beer, and Bratwurst.

2. Formally known as Persia, this country can be found in Asia.
a. Afghanistan   b. Syria   c. Pakistan   d. Iran

3. This country is bordered by Myanmar, Laos, Cambodia and Malaysia.
a. Vietnam   b. Thailand   c. Bhutan   d. Bangladesh

4. This country is home to the CN Tower, Lake Louise and Chateau Frontenac.

5. This country was previously known as Burma.
a. Malaysia   b. India   c. Mongolia   d. Myanmar

6. This country is known for the best safaris, is home to the Big Five, has 50 epic national parks, and has a population of 57 million as of 2023.
a. South Africa   b. Ghana   c. Central African Republic   d. Kenya

7. Gold medal winner, Usain Bolt, is from this country.

8. This country is the second most biodiverse country in the world after Brazil.
a. China   b. Colombia   c. Peru   d. Mexico

9. This country has the highest GDP per capita as of 2023 and has a population of roughly 3 million.

10. Which European country is bordered by seven countries including Poland, Slovakia, Hungary and Belarus?

11. The capital of this country is Kabul.
a. Syria   b. Afghanistan   c. Iran   d. Lebanon

12. Name of the country where vodka originated from.

13. In this country you will find the islands of Crete and Corfu.

14. Located in Europe, this country was Hans Christian Andersen's birthplace.
a. Denmark   b. Norway   c. Sweden   d. Finland

15. Excluding Hong Kong (which is the highest, but not an official country), which country has the highest life expectancy at 85.03 years?
a. Switzerland   b. Japan   c. Macau   d. Singapore

16. A country lying just north of the equator, you would travel here to see the Batu Caves.

17. This country is home to the cities of Fez and Casablanca.

18. Found in South America, this country is known for its coffee and its vast grasslands called Los Llanos.
a. Venezuela   b. Uruguay   c. Colombia   d. Chile

19. The capital city of this country is Yaoundé.

20. Which country is nicknamed the Pearl of the Indian Ocean and the Teardrop of India?

21. Which European country is bordered by Austria, Germany, Poland, and Slovakia?
a. Netherlands   b. hungary   c. Czech Republic   d. Estonia

22. In this country you will find the cities of Manchester and Oxford.

23. This small country is an enclave of South Africa.

24. Here you will find the Northern Lights, Blue Lagoon, volcanoes, and glaciers.

25. Where can you find the world's most famous canal, which is an artificial 82 km long waterway connecting the Pacific and Atlantic Oceans?

26. This country is bordered by Iraq, the Persian Gulf, and Saudi Arabia.
a. Israel   b. Jordan   c. Kuwait   d. Qatar

27. I'm standing at Lake Bled, which country am I in?

28. Which country has both a Greek side and a Turkish side?

29. This country in Asia is also known as the Vegas of the East.

30. Budapest is the capital of this country.

MOUNTAINS

1. What mountain range runs through Switzerland, Austria, France, and Italy?

2. The Sugar Loaf mountain is located in which country in South America?

3. The Pyrenees mountain range forms the border between which two countries?

4. Mount Elbert is the highest mountain in which mountain range?
a. Sierra Nevada   b. Andes
c. Atlas Mountains   d. Rocky Mountains

5. Surprisingly, Everest is not the tallest mountain when measured from base to peak, but rather this title goes to Mauna Kea in Hawaii. How tall does this mountain measure from the sea bed to the summit?
a. 9,245 m   b. 10,210 m   c. 11,345 m   d. 12,790 m

6. What is the exact height of Mount Everest?
a. 7,724 m   b. 8,207 m   c. 8,849 m   d. 9330 m

7. The Appalachian Mountains run down which cost in America?
a. West coast   b. East coast   c. North coast   d. South coast

8. Seven states can be seen from which US mountain in Alabama?

9. The Ural Mountains separate which two continents?

10. The Appalachian Mountain range covers which three countries?

11. Gangkhar Puensum is the highest unclimbed mountain in the world. Where can you find this mountain?
a. Nepal   b. China   c. India   d. Bhutan

12. Mount Kilimanjaro is the tallest mountain in Africa, but in which country would you find it?
a. Kenya   b. Tanzania   c. Ethiopia   d. Mozambique

13. What is the highest mountain in the United Kingdom?

14. The Seven Summits are comprised of the highest mountain on all seven continents. Many of these mountains have already been discussed in this book, but how many of them can you name? (In some continents it is up for debate which mountains count, so multiple answers to some continents will be given in the answers)

15. Mont Blanc is the tallest mountain in the alps, but just how high is it?
a. 4,810 m   b. 5,045 m   c. 5,390 m   d. 5,602 m

16. What is the name of the person who free soloed (climbed without ropes) El Capitan in Yosemite National Park, resulting in the documentary Free Solo being made in 2018?

17. What is the second-highest mountain on Earth?
a. Lhotse   b. K2   c. Makalu   d. Cho Oyu

18. Mount Elbert can be found in which state?
a. Maine   b. Arizona   c. Colorado   d. Illinois

19. In which country would you find Mount Fuji?
a. Japan   b. South Korea   c. Indonesia   d. Afghanistan

20. What is the name of the Himalayan mountain with the highest fatality rate at 32%, causing over 60 people to lose their lives?

21. On average, how many people each year die climbing Mount Everest?
a. 5   b. 9   c. 15   d. 24

22. Mount Snowden can be found in which country?
a. England   b. Wales   c. Scotland   d. Northern Ireland

23. In which country can the Laurentian Mountains be found?

24. Where can the Mons Huygens mountain be located?

25. Who were the first people to climb Mount Everest?

26. In which year was Everest first climbed?
a. 1950   b. 1953   c. 1956   d. 1959

27. Zugspitze is the tallest mountain in which European country?
a. Austria   b. Switzerland   c. Liechtenstein   d. Germany

28. Edward Whymper first climbed which iconic Swiss mountain in 1865?

29. Where can the highest mountain in our solar system be found?
a. Earth   b. Mars   c. Neptune   d. Pluto

30. What is the highest mountain in New Zealand?

Historical Geography

1. Sri Lanka was previously known as what?

2. In which year did Persia change its name to Iran?
a. 1925   b. 1935   c. 1945   d. 1955

3. In which year did Siam change its name to Thailand?
a. 1939   b. 1949   c. 1959   d. 1969

4. What was the supercontinent that existed during the late Paleozoic and early Mesozoic eras called?

5. After colonialism, Southern Rhodesia became Zimbabwe. What did Northern Rhodesia become?
a. Zambia   b. Botswana   c. Malawi   d. Zimbabwe

6. What was the capital city of the Byzantine Empire?

7. Why did The Republic of Macedonia change to the Republic of North Macedonia?

8. In which year did the Czech Republic officially change its name to Czechia?
a. 2010   b. 2016   c. 2022   d. It hasn't

9. Yugoslavia was a country in Southeast Europe and Central Europe. What 6 countries made up Yugoslavia?

10. Swaziland changed its name in 2018 to what?

11. Name the ancient city which was destroyed by a volcano in 79 AD.

12. To celebrate the 20th anniversary of its independence, the Republic of Upper Volta changed its name to what?
a. Sierra Leone   b. Burkina Faso   c. Mali   d. Niger

13. What is the name of the ancient city, which is carved out of rock, and can be found in Jordan?

14. Saigon was renamed after being captured by North Vietnamese troops. What is the city now called?

15. The Spice Islands were once highly sought-after islands. What are these islands known as today?

16. What was the capital of the Incan Empire?
a. Ingapirca   b. Chan Chan   c. Pisac   d. Cusco

17. The Ming Dynasty are responsible for building which architectural marvel between 1368-1644?

18. Namibia's new name was decided by the UN and changed in 1990. What did Namibia use to be called?
a. French South West Africa   b. German South West Africa
c. Spanish South West Africa   d. British South West Africa

19. The capital of China, Beijing, used to be called something else. What name did it have?
a. Peking   b. Nanjing   c. Hangzhou   d. Anyang

20. Tanganyika and Zanzibar formed to make which country in 1964?
a. Djibouti   b. Kiribati   c. Tanzania   d. Mauritius

21. The oldest known pyramid in Egypt was built in 2630 BC, but what is its name?
a. The Great Pyramid   b. Step Pyramid   c. Pyramid of Khafre

22. What was Ethiopia's previous name before it was changed in 1945?
a. Abyssinia   b. Obyssinia   c. Indysinnia   d. Thanysinnia

23. In which year did Kenya become independent?
a. 1945   b. 1955   c. 1963   d. 1971

24. Name the ancient civilisation that built Machu Picchu in modern-day Peru.

25. Which countries occupied Germany after World War 2?

26. In which year did Apartheid officially end in South Africa?
a. 1992   b. 1994   c. 1996   d. 1998

27. In which year did the berlin wall fall?
a. 1986   b. 1987   c. 1988   d. 1989

28. Which of the following was the capital city of the Mongol Empire from 1235 - 1260?
a. Sarai   b. Karakorum   c. Yingchang   d. Zhongdu

29. Which city did Alfred the Great make the capital of England in 871 AD?
a. Wessex   b. Chester   c. Canterburry   d. Winchester

30. In which year did Canberra become the capital of Australia?
a. 1908   b. 1932   c. 1948   d. 1961

TOURISM

1. Can you list the top ten countries with the most tourists as of 2019?

2. Roughly how many planes are in the air at any given time?
a. 36,000   b. 9,000   c. 4,000   d. 18,000

3. Who is known as the Father of Tourism?
a. William Boeing   b. Harrison Ford
c. Thomas Cook   d. Christopher Colombus

4. How long is the world's shortest commercial flight?
a. 40 minutes   b. 10 seconds   c. 12 minutes   d. 2 minutes

5. Which country has the most powerful passport in the world, which allows its nationals to visit 193 destinations visa-free?
a. Singapore   b. Australia   c. Tuvalu   d. Japan

6. The two European countries with the most powerful passports are third on the list globally, with 190 visa-free destinations. Which countries are they?
a. Monaco and Austria   b. France and Switzerland
c. UK and Ireland   d. Germany and Spain

7. Roughly how many tourism-related jobs were lost during the pandemic worldwide?
a. 31 million   b. 62 million   c. 10 million   d. 140 million

8. How many airports does London have?
a. 4   b. 5   c. 6   d. 7

9. What is the most visited country in South America?
a. Colombia   b. Peru   c. Brazil   d. Argentina

10. Which of the following foods was an essential material used in the construction of the Great Wall of China?
a. Curry   b. Lychees   c. Sticky Rice   d. Porridge

11. Travelling for leisure for the general public was popularised during which global event?
a. WW1   b. The decline of the British Empire
c. The Cold War   d. The Industrial Revolution

12. You could book an airbnb in 98% of the world, with the exceptions of North Korea, Crimea, Syria and which other country?
a. Iran   b. Somalia   c. Guinea-Bissau   d. Yemen

13. In 2019, the country that visited the US the most was Canada, followed by Mexico, followed by the UK. Which country came fourth?
a. China   b. Japan   c. France   d. Brazil

14. True or false: it is possible to visit Pyongyang, in North Korea, as a tourist.

15. Tourism, as we know it today, can trace its origins back to an expedition taken by European upper-class men between the 17th and 19th centuries. What was this called?
a. The Great Adventure   b. The Grand Tour
c. The Men's Journey   d. The Long Trip

16. What was the most visited national park in the US in 2022?
a. Yellowstone National Park
b. Grand Canyon National Park
c. Rocky Mountain National Park
d. Great Smoky Mountains National Park

17. How many European countries could you visit with an Interrail pass?
a. 8   b. 19   c. 25   d. 33

18. What percentage of Americans have visited at least 10 countries?
a. 11%   b. 28%   c. 44%   d. 65%

19. How many listings are on Airbnb as of 2023?
a. 800,000+   b. 3 million+   c. 6 million+   d. 15 million+

20. Which Caribbean island is the most visited by tourists?
a. Puerto Rico   b. Dominican Republic   c. The Bahamas

21. Tens of millions of people visit the UK each year, but which country out of Wales and Scotland are visited more by tourists?

22. How many European countries do not have an airport?
a. 0   b. 1   c. 5   d. 10

23. True or false: flying can impact your smell and taste by 30%.

24. The vast majority (43%) of cruise-goers are from which country?
a. China   b. India   c. US   d. UK

25. Which city has the most hotels?
a. New York   b. London   c. Beijing   d. Tokyo

26. Which country has the highest number of visitors going on ski holidays?
a. France   b. Austria   c. Japan   d. United States

27. What is the least visited country in the world as of 2023?
a. Togo   b. Tuvalu   c. Lesotho   d. San Marino

28. On average, how many holidays in America are via road trip?
a. 1 in 3   b. 1 in 5   c. 1 in 10   d. 1 in 20

29. What is the most popular holiday destination for Brits?
a. Spain   b. France   c. Portugal   d. US

30. True or false: Global Tourism is the largest industry in the world.

NAME THE TOURIST ATTRACTION AND LOCATION

31. The largest amphitheatre in the world, which was built between 72 AD and 80 AD.

32. This performing arts facility, which was opened in 1973, is the most well-known building in the whole continent.

33. This European museum is the largest and most visited in the world. It is also home to what is, arguably, the most famous painting in the world.

34. The residence of the Pope which is decorated with art from the Renaissance. It is home to the most famous ceiling in the world.

35. You can find this reminder of the Incan Empire in the Andes.

36. This temple can be found in South East Asia and is believed to be the largest religious structure on earth.

37. This 'Lost City' of 312BC is built into sand and stone and can be found in the Middle East.

38. This humongous chasm is larger than the state of Rhode Island.

39. This city is home to the tallest twin skyscrapers, which share their name with an oil and gas company.

40. This statue of a religious figure is nearly 100 feet tall and has become symbolic of an entire nation.

41. This famous bell tower is at a 4-degree angle.

42. This is the largest building in the world, at 2700 feet.

43. This monument symbolises the reunification of Germany.

44. This tourist hotspot is a green centrepiece to one of the busiest cities in the world and is larger than Monaco, and gets over 40 million visitors annually.

45. This South-East Asian island is known for its rice fields, buzzing nightlife and spiritual retreats, and is the only Hindu-majority province in the country.

46. This prehistoric monument is believed to have been built from around 3000 BC to 2000 BC. It consists of an outer ring of large freestanding stones, with a ring of smaller bluestones inside.

47. Tourists visit this building to appreciate its rich history and also to witness the guards who surround the building and wear tall, black fur caps.

48. This area is the heart of a bustling city which is known for jazz, Mardi Gras, and for being a melting pot of American, African and French influences, and was founded by the French in 1718.

49. This European island is a honeymooners hotspot and is known for white buildings upon a volcanic rock.

50. The world's largest salt flat is found here.

GUESS THE CITY

(NON-CAPITALS)

1. This transcontinental country is known for its Islamic architecture and stray cats.

2. This European city is a UNESCO World Heritage Site and is featured in Game of Thrones. Tourists could take a day trip to Montenegro if they fancied it.

3. The annual Oktoberfest festival is held here.

4. The city is home to the Golden Gate Bridge.

5. This city is known as the birthplace of the Industrial Revolution. Nowadays, it is a trendy and buzzy alternative for those who choose not to live in London.

6. This European city is a financial hub and home to the United Nations, Red Cross, The World Health Organization and many more.

7. Think deep-dish pizzas and 1920's gangsters.

8. Sometimes known as Sin City, this hub of nightlife is found in the middle of the desert.

9. This is the largest city in this country despite not being a capital and is the homeplace of Drake, Jim Carrey, Mike Myers and Keanu Reeves.

10. This city is known for being a centre for Islam through many African empires. It was an important trading hub throughout history and was sometimes called 'The City of Gold'.

11. This city is often mistaken for this African country's capital and was the home of Nelson Mandela when he died.

12. This city faces the Atlantic Ocean and boasts a mixture of Moorish and French architecture due to its colonial history.

13. This is the most populous city in West Africa, with over 10 million citizens.

14. Found near the Yangtze River, this is one of the largest cities in the world. It is home to The Bund and Yu Garden.

15. This city was previously known as Bombay.

16. The capital of this Asian country is Sri Jayawardenepura Kotte despite the fact that this large city is more well-known.

17. This Asian city was renamed to honour the leader of its revolution.

18. This South American city is famous for its colourful annual street parades.

19. This Australasian city is one of the most isolated in the world, with a vast outback on one side and the Indian Ocean on the other.

20. This city is known as the City of Sails and has the highest Polynesian population in the world.

LANGUAGES

1. What is considered to be the Mother of all Languages?
a. Sanskrit   b. Latin   c. Arabic   d. Tamil

2. What percentage of the world is bilingual?
a. 12%   b. 25%   c. 43%   d. 64%

3. Name the country with the most languages in the world, with its nationals speaking more than 800 languages.
a. India   b. Indonesia   c. Philippines   d. Papua New Guinea

4. What is the fastest spoken language in the world?
a. Japanese   b. Spanish   c. Mandarin   d. Russian

5. Despite the fact that there are 6500 languages on earth, 97% of the population speak just this percentage of them.
a. 20%   b. 9%   c. 4%   d. 0.5%

6. Excluding Russian, what is the most common native language in Europe?
a. French   b. Spanish   c. English   d. German

7. Mandarin has 4 tones, how many does Cantonese have?
a. 1   b. 2   c. 6   d. 9

8. Despite the fact that this is considered a 'dead language', it is learned by nearly 2 million people worldwide.

9. Which language has the longest alphabet in the world?
a. Greek   b. Farsi   c. Swedish   d. Khmer

10. Which of the following is a Romance language?
a. English   b. Romanian   c. Yiddish   d. Faroese

11. Afrikaans is spoken in South Africa, Namibia, Botswana, Zambia and Zimbabwe. Which language is it derived from?

12. Which language does the word 'alphabet' derive from?
a. Greek   b. Latin   c. Sanskrit   d. Arabic

13. As of 2023, what is the third most translated text in the world?
a. The Bible   b. Harry Potter and the Sorcerer's Stone
c. The Quran   d. Pinocchio

14. The English alphabet has 26 letters and how many sounds?
a. 55   b. 44   c. 22   d. 11

15. What is the largest French-speaking city in the world?
a. Marseille, France   b. Kinshasa, Democratic Republic of the Congo
c. Paris, France   d. Abidjan, Ivory Coast

16. What is the national language of The Philippines?

17. Which country has the most official languages in the world (37)?
a. Indonesia   b. The United States   c. Bolivia   d. India

18. Many languages have genders masculine and feminine, and some have a third. What is it known as?

19. True or false: Nigeria has more English speakers than England.

20. Spanish is the official language in how many countries?
a. 33   b. 14   c. 5   d. 20

POLITICAL GEOGRAPHY

1. How many countries are in the Commonwealth?
a. 21   b. 39   c. 54   d. 72

2. What was the first country to become independent in the 20th century?
a. Australia   b. Canada   c. India   d. Jamaica

3. Which European country does Greenland belong to?
a. Denmark   b. Norway   c. Sweden   d. Finland

4. Which country became independent from Indonesia in 2002?
a. Papua New Guinea   b. East Timor   c. Tuvalu   d. Fiji

5. The Partition commonly refers to the independence of a nation and the creation of another. Which nations are they?

6. Which of the following countries is not a member of the EU?
a. Estonia   b. Poland   c. Norway   d. Slovenia

7. In which country would you find Strasbourg, a city which is historically German-speaking?
a. Austria   b. France   c. Switzerland   d. Belgium

8. The acquisition of Alaska was sold for the bargain price of how many cents per acre?
a. 80   b. 25   c. 2   d. 0.2

9. Name the continental invasion in which European powers divided up African countries amongst themselves.

10. Name the group of European islands off the coast of Western Sahara.
a. Canary Islands   b. Cook Islands   c. Solomon Islands

11. The Republic of Suriname became independent from which nation in 1975?
a. Belgium   b. Spain   c. Portugal   d. Netherlands

12. The handover of this island to China in 1997 has signalled unrest in its population.

13. The collapse of the USSR resulted in the emergence of how many post-Soviet countries?
a. 6   b. 9   c. 12   d. 15

14. How many countries have claimed independence from The British Empire or the UK?
a. 35   b. 50   c. 65   d. 80

15. As of 2022, what is the most recent country to have separated into two countries?

16. Name the Pacific island which is still under occupation after an illegal coup in 1893 ousted their native government.

17. Name the British Overseas Territory which can be found at the very tip of the Iberian Peninsula.
a. Falkland Islands   b. Cayman Islands   c. Gibraltar   d. Bermuda

18. Which organisation was once known as EEC until 1993?

19. Which English county is fighting for its independence, and has its own language which is spoken fluently by approximately 300 people?
a. Cornwall   b. Devon   c. Yorkshire   d. Dorset

20. Which American state declared independence from Mexico in 1836?
a. California   b. Arizona   c. Texas   d. New Mexico

TERMINOLOGY

CAN YOU GIVE THE GEOGRAPHIC TERM FOR THESE DEFINITIONS?

1. A body of water which is long, narrow and reaches far inland. Norway has many, as does Chile, Canada and New Zealand.

2. Measured in degrees, this is the distance either north or south of the equator.
a. Latitude   b. Longitude

3. A man-made waterway built for transport, irrigation and trade.

4. An area just outside of a city which is mostly residential.

5. A large cluster of islands.

6. Measured in degrees, this is the distance east to west.
a. Latitude   b. Longitude

7. An area of salt-water which is separated from the sea from a coral reef or sandbar.

8. A hot spring which can erupt and send hot water into the air.

9. The science of map-making.
a. Papography   b. Terrainography
c. Topography   d. Cartography

10. Two parts of the earth that are diametrically opposite.
a. Antisides   b. Antipodes   c. Antilines   d. Antimones

11. A passage of water which separates two oceans or seas.

12. Height in relation to sea or ground level.

13. A muddy or sandy area where the river meets the sea. They are often triangular.

14. An area where a freshwater river meets the ocean.

15. This is where the longitude is widely acknowledged to be 0 degrees and passes through Greenwich, England.

16. An area of grassy plain which has few trees and is often found in Africa.

17. A large inlet of the ocean which extends into the land.

18. An imaginary line which divides the Earth in two.

19. A territory with borders surrounded entirely by one other territory.

20. A thin piece of land which is connected to the mainland but mainly surrounded by water.

NATURAL DISASTERS

1. What is the name of the scale used to measure the strength of earthquakes, which was devised in 1935?

2. Despite speculation surrounding the accurate numbers, it is said that the deadliest natural disaster, which killed up to 4 million people, was a flood that occurred in which country in 1931?

3. Which of the following is not a type of volcanic eruption?
a. Strombolian   b. Plinian   c. Morphian   d. Pelean

4. Which country did a catastrophic earthquake hit on the 12th of January 2010, resulting in a death toll of 100,000 - 316,000?

5. The largest ever earthquake was recorded in Chile in 1960, but what did this 'megaquake' record on the scale from question 1?
a. 9   b. 9.2   c. 9.3   d. 9.5

6. What is the most common type of natural disaster, resulting in 43% of all natural disasters since 2006?
a. Earthquake   b. Floods   c. Tsunami   d. Hurricane

7. True or false: Hurricanes usually last a much shorter time than tornadoes, with wind speeds far greater than that of tornadoes.

8. The largest tsunami ever recorded hit the banks of Lituya Bay in Southeast Alaska in 1958, but just how tall was the wave?
a. 225 m   b. 325 m   c. 425 m   d. 525 m

9. In which country did Cyclone Nargis occur in 2008, which killed approximately 138,000 people?
a. Mauritania   b. Belize   c. Myanmar   d. Togo

10. The 2004 Boxing Day Tsunami was one of the deadliest natural disasters in history, with Indonesia, Sri Lanka, and India reporting the most fatalities. How many people tragically lost their lives to this tsunami?
a. 158,000   b. 228,000   c. 319,000   d. 468,000

11. True or false: hurricanes usually form over the ocean.

12. Approximately how many years ago did Yellowstone last erupt?
a. 70,000   b. 100,000   c. 140,000   d. 190,000

13. What is the name of the Indonesian volcano which erupted in 1883, resulting in the death of over 36,000 people?

14. Nevado del Ruiz erupted in 1985, resulting in the death of 23,000 people. In which country did this strategy occur?
a. Venezuela   b. Spain   c. Peru   d. Colombia

15. What is the name for the movement of rocks or debris down a slope?

16. What is the name of a deep open crack which you find in glaciers, which has claimed the lives of hundreds of mountaineers over time?

17. Which type of volcanic flow is described by the following statement: a fast-moving current of volcanic matter, hot gas and ash, that travels at a speed of over 10 metres per second.

18. More than 8,000 people were killed in the deadliest natural disaster to ever affect the US, but what was it and where did it happen?

19. What is the name for the rapid movement of snow and ice down a slope?

20. Nearly 40% of all hurricanes to hit the US from the year 1851 have hit the same state, but which state is this?
a. Louisiana   b. Texas   c. North Carolina   d. Florida

21. True or false: the majority of wildfires in the US are caused naturally.

22. The 1973 Luhuo earthquake is one of the deadliest in history, reportedly killing over 2 million people, but in which country did this occur?
a. Pakistan   b. Bangladesh   c. China   d. India

23. The 1920s was one of the worst decades on record for fatalities caused by natural disasters, with 524,000 people dying on average across the world annually from natural disasters. 472,000 of these were just one type of natural disaster, but which one was it?
a. Earthquakes   b. Floods   c. Drought   d. Extreme temperatures

24. What is the name given to the string of volcanoes around the edge of the Pacific Ocean?
a. Crescent of Chaos   b. Ring of Fire   c. Circle of Destruction

25. Roughly what percent of earthquakes occur within this area of the Pacific Ocean?
a. 40%   b. 60%   c. 75%   d. 90%

26. Name the flu which is responsible for killing a reported 50 million people between 1918-1920.

27. In which century was the black death most prevalent, killing 75 - 200 million people?
a. 13th   b. 14th   c. 15th   d. 16th

28. Name the plague responsible for killing 30 - 50 million people in Europe and West Asia from 541 AD - 542 AD.

29. Which disease is responsible for killing 5 - 8 million people in Mexico from 1519 - 1520?

30. Name the plague of AD 165 to 180 which had a devastating effect on the Roman Empire, killing 5 - 10 million people.

CLIMATE CHANGE

1. What is the main greenhouse gas responsible for climate change?
a. Carbon monoxide   b. Carbon dioxide   c. Carbon nitrate

2. Despite this gas having a devastating effect on the climate, most of the atmosphere is made up of nitrogen and oxygen, but just how much of the atmosphere is made up of these two gasses?
a. 90%   b. 95%   c. 98%   d. 99%

3. Approximately how much has the earth's average global temperature risen since 1880?
a. 0.5°C   b. 0.8°C   c. 1.5°C   d. 2.5°C

4. How much have sea levels risen since 1900?
a. 5 cm   b. 21 cm   c. 65 cm   d. 120 cm

5. Which global climate agreement did the United States withdraw from in 2020, only to rejoin again in 2021?

6. The target of this agreement is to limit the rise in future global mean temperature to 1.5°C above pre-industrial levels. How much do they estimate that emissions need to be cut by 2030 in order to achieve this?
a. 20%   b. 35%   c. 50%   d. 70%

7. Which of the following was the main cause of the depletion of the ozone layer?
a. nitrogen oxides   b. sulfur oxides
c. Chlorofluorocarbons (CFCs)   d. Methane gas

8. The largest hole in the ozone layer is 24.5 million km^2, but over which area would you find it?
a. Greenland   b. Antarctica   c. Alaska   d. Australia

9. Excluding microplastic, how many pieces of plastic are there in the ocean?
a. 50 billion   b. 500 billion   c. 2 trillion   d. 5 trillion

10. True or false: climate change has no impact on the number of tropical storms.

11. What is the geographical term for something that absorbs more carbon from the atmosphere than it releases?

12. The Amazon rainforest has shrunk by approximately 13%, with one industry being responsible for about 80% of all deforestation. Which industry is this?
a. Palm oil   b. Logging   c. Cattle   d. Mining

13. How much of American energy comes from renewable energy sources?
a. 5%   b. 12%   c. 20%   d. 33%

14. True or false: melting permafrost could have a devastating effect on the climate as they are a great storage of carbon dioxide.

15. Approximately how many species are believed to have gone extinct since 1900?
a. 250   b. 500   c. 1000   d. 2000

16. Which country is the largest emitter of greenhouse gases today?
a. China   b. US   c. India   d. Brazil

17. Three of the following countries still allow the commercial hunting of whales. Which three are they?
a. China   b. Russia   c. Japan   d. Finland   e. Norway   f. Iceland

18. Coral is very susceptible to changes in sea temperature. How much of the world's coral did we lose from 2008 - 2019 as a result of the sea temperature rising?
a. 4%   b. 7%   c. 11%   d. 14%

19. According to the UNHCR, how many people have been displaced annually by weather-related events since 2008?
a. 3 million   b. 8.5 million   c. 14 million   d. 21.5 million

20. How much has the Argentière Glacier (a glacier on Mont Blanc) retreated since 1870?
a. 300 m   b. 550 m   c. 850 m   d. 1,150 m

OCEANS AND SEAS

1. What percent of the earth's surface is covered by water?
a. 61%   b. 66%   c. 71%   d. 76%

2. What percent of the earth's water is held in oceans?
a. 91%   b. 93.5%   c. 96.5%   d. 99%

3. Which ocean is both the largest and the deepest?

4. What is the name of the deepest part of the ocean, and in which trench can it be found?

5. How deep is this deepest part of the ocean?
a. 10,935 m   b. 11,623 m   c. 12,704 m   d. 13,449 m

6. Which ocean has the longest coastline?
a. Indian Ocean   b. Pacific Ocean
c. Actic Ocean   d. Atlantic Ocean

7. Historically there have been 4 oceans, being the Arctic Ocean, the Indian Ocean, the Pacific Ocean and the Atlantic Ocean, however, most countries including the United States now recognise a fifth ocean. What is it called?

8. What is the average depth of the world's oceans?
a. 2,700 m   b. 3,700 m   c. 4,700 m   d. 5,700 m

9. Which of the following seas lies between Asia and Europe, and is bounded by Romania, Russia, Turkey, Georgia, Ukraine and Bulgaria?
a. Sargasso Sea   b. Black Sea   c. Coral Sea   d. Weddell Sea

10. Name the sea which is off the eastern and south-eastern coasts of Spain.

11. Which ocean would you find at the northernmost point of the earth?

12. Name the largest landlocked sea in the world.

13. Between which two countries is the Tasman Sea located?

14. Covering approximately 20% of the earth's surface, which ocean is the second largest in the world?

15. Which manmade waterway connects the Pacific and Atlantic Oceans?

16. Name the island in the Atlantic Ocean where the North American and Eurasian tectonic plates meet.

17. How many oceans does the US border?
a. 1   b. 2   c. 3   d. 4

18. The island of Madagascar is surrounded by which ocean?

19. In which ocean do you find the huge majority of oceans?

20. The Gulf Stream is a warm ocean current that passes through which ocean?

21. According to the World Register of Marine Species, how many marine species are currently known to us?
a. 10,000   b. 110,000   c. 240,000   d. 710,000

22. True or false: the Great Barrier Reef is the largest coral reef on earth.

23. What percent of the world's oceans are currently protected?
a. 7%   b. 18%   c. 32%   d. 48%

24. The Great Pacific Garbage Patch is the largest garbage patch on earth, but roughly how does its size compare to that of France?
a. Half the size   b. The same size
c. Twice the size   d. Triple the size

25. How many oceans does the equator run through?
a. 1   b. 2   c. 3   d. 4

26. Which ocean does the Amazon River run into?

27. The longest mountain range in the world amazingly runs along the sea floor, and is called the mid-ocean ridge. Just how long is this range?
a. 30,000 km   b. 45,000 km   c. 65,000 km   d. 90,000 km

28. What percent of the world's oceans have been explored and charted by humans?
a. 5%   b. 10%   c. 17%   d. 26%

29. Phytoplankton in the ocean among other things are very large contributors to producing the planet's oxygen. Just how much of the planet's oxygen does the ocean produce?
a. 12%   b. 24%   c. 38%   d. 50%

30. True or false: there are more stars in our galaxy than there is plastic in the ocean.

GEOLOGY

1. According to the Mohs scale, what is the hardest mineral on the planet?
a. Diamond   b. Topaz   c. Corundum   d. Quartz

2. There are three main types of rock. Two of these are sedimentary and igneous, but what is the third?

3. Which of these three types of rocks is formed when lava cools?

4. Which mineral is better known as fool's gold, due to its deceptive gold appearance?

5. What is the name of the icicle-shaped formation that hangs from cave ceilings, and is produced from the minerals in dripping water?

6. Into which type of rock is the Mount Rushmore structure carved?
a. Limestone   b. Granite   c. Basalt   d. Anthracite

7. Seismology is the scientific name given to the study of what?

8. Which of the three main types of rock is best for finding fossils?

9. What is the name of the spiral-shaped fossil, which is one of the most common fossils that one can find?
a. Devil's toenails   b. Ammonites   c. Belemnites   d. Brachiopods

10. What is the name of the fossilised tree resin, which is very popular in jewellery?

11. What colour are emeralds?
a. Blue   b. Pink   c. Clear   d. Green

12. 90% of Europe's natural slate used for roofing comes from which European country?
a. Italy   b. Portugal   c. Spain   d. Ireland

13. Sapphires and rubies are both varieties of the same mineral. Which mineral is this?
a. Corundum   b. Amphibole   c. Calcite

14. The earth's crust is divided into two types: oceanic crust and what else?

15. What is the term used for the study of fossils?

1. The following four countries all rank among the top 10 countries in the world for the highest GDP per capita. Put them in order of highest GDP per capita to lowest: Switzerland, Ireland, Luxembourg, and Singapore.

2. What was the unemployment rate in the US in January 2023?
a. 2.6%   b. 3.6%   c. 4.6%   d. 5.6%

3. It is well known that the racial wealth gap in America is still extremely high. How much higher is the median net worth of white households compared to that of black households?
a. 2 times   b. 4 times   c. 7 times   d. 10 times

4. Which country has the highest average salary for teachers?
a. Monaco   b. Luxembourg   c. UAE   d. Qatar

5. The United States and China dominate the countries by GDP list, but which country has a higher GDP?

6. To the nearest trillion dollars, what was the total GDP of the USA in 2022?
a. $13 trillion   b. $21 trillion   c. $29 trillion   d. $40 trillion

7. Which country is third on the highest GDP list?
a. Germany   b. UK   c. India   d. Japan

8. Which country is home to the most billionaires as of 2022?

9. America tops the list of most female billionaires, but what percentage of their total billionaires do they make up?
a. 8%   b. 13%   c. 18%   d. 23%

10. Which US state is home to the most billionaires?
a. New York   b. Florida   c. Texas   d. California

11. The international poverty line was updated in September 2022. What was it increased to?
a. $2.15   b. $3.46   c. $4.79   d. $6.02

12. What percent of the global population lives under the poverty line, and are therefore considered to be living in extreme poverty?
a. 4%   b. 8%   c. 14%   d. 20%

13. What percent of the global population lives on less than $6.85 per day?
a. 30%   b. 40%   c. 50%   d. 60%

14. What is the federal minimum wage in America as of January 2023?
a. $7.25   b. $8.75   c. $9.90   d. $11.05

15. Between the years of 2010 to 2018, how much tax on their annual income did the wealthiest 400 families in America pay?
a. 8.2%   b. 13.1%   c. 18.7%   d. 23.9%

16. Brazil has the highest GDP of South American countries, but which country has the second highest?
a. Colombia   b. Peru   c. Argentina   d. Chile

17. Which of the following is the largest global industry by revenue in 2023?
a. Global Pension Funds
b. Global Car & Automobile Sales
c. Global Life & Health Insurance Carriers
d. Global Commercial Real Estate

18. What is the average salary in the UK as of January 2023?
a. £29,600   b. £34,800   c. £39,100   d. £43,100

19. What is the term used to describe the number of services or goods that a certain amount of money will buy at any given time?

20. Approximately how much has the stock market gone up on average over the last century?
a. 5%   b. 10%   c. 16%   d. 22%

ANAGRAM ROUND

THE FOLLOWING WILL BE 10 ANAGRAMS OF COUNTRIES.
HOW MANY CAN YOU GET?

1. Erny gam
2. Azana tin
3. Alaris uta
4. Deni sonia
5. Mice ox
6. Busk zeatin
7. Carious haft
8. Aile gar
9. Alis maya
10. Alic end

THE FOLLOWING WILL BE 10 ANAGRAMS OF US STATES.
HOW MANY CAN YOU GET?

1. Cent octunci
2. Ania ind
3. Abe snark
4. Andros delhi
5. Scions win
6. Ese sennet
7. Alvan spinney
8. Hoot tankard
9. Cominx wee
10. Atman no

THE FOLLOWING WILL BE 10 ANAGRAMS OF CAPITAL CITIES. HOW MANY CAN YOU GET?

1. Change peon
2. Raw was
3. A butchers
4. Jab lulanj
5. Inge jib
6. Agnes pori
7. A rico
8. Lentil wong
9. Ai hon
10. Ailis bar

POPULATION STATS

1. What percent of the global population lives in Europe?
a. 10%   b. 14%   c. 18%   d. 22%

2. What percentage of the population lives in the southern hemisphere?
a. 10%   b. 18%   c. 24%   d. 30%

3. According to the 2021 Census, what percentage of the population in the UK is white?
a. 43%   b. 54%   c. 68%   d. 82%

4. What percentage of the population in the US is Hispanic?
a. 11%   b. 19%   c. 25%   d. 32%

5. What percentage of the population in Canada has French as their native language?
a. 5%   b. 12%   c. 23%   d. 42%

6. What percentage of Australians are indigenous Aboriginals?
a. 3.3%   b. 6%   c. 10%   d. 14%

7. Germans nationals make up 86.3% of the population in Germany. Which nationality is second, at 1.8%?

8. Which country in the United Kingdom is the least densely populated?

9. Roughly what percentage of the world are vegetarian?
a. 7%   b. 14%   c. 22%   d. 35%

10. Roughly what percentage of Africa identifies as Christian as of 2020?
a. 28%   b. 35%   c. 41%   d. 49%

1. It is no surprise that the United States has the most McDonald's, but just how many is it home to?
a. 6,000   b. 10,000   c. 14,000   d. 20,000

2. The Maglev Bullet Train is the fastest in the world at 375 miles per hour. Which country can you find it in?

3. True or false: By surface area, the dwarf planet Pluto can fit in Russia.

4. True or false: Dogs are banned in Antarctica.

5. True or false: The current year in Ethiopia is 2015.

6. Name the Central American country that does not have an army.
a. El Salvador   b. Costa Rica   c. Belize   d. Dominican Republic

7. Which European country is known as the land of no surnames?

8. The top 5 busiest airports of 2022 by the number of flights were all located in which country?

9. Which country has the most Michelin-star restaurants in the world with 628?
a. United States   b. China   c. Italy   d. France

10. How many people who live in Monaco are millionaires?
a 1 in 10   b. 1 in 5   c. 1 in 3   d. 1 in 2

11. True or false: Jet lag is worse from east to west.

12. How many beaches does Australia have?
a. 12,000   b. 7000   c. 4000   d. 800

13. Which city has the most bridges in the world with over 2300?
a. Venice   b. Prague   c. Hamburg   d. London

14. Which country was once known as the Iberian Union?
a. Turkey   b. Portugal   c. Spain   d. Russia

15. Which American state has a larger population than Canada?

16. What is the only continent to cover all four hemispheres?

17. Which Asian country was named after a Spanish King?
a. Mongolia   b. Cambodia   c. Philippines   d. Vietnam

18. How many countries in Central Asia end with the suffix 'stan'?
a. 5   b. 7   c. 9   d. 11

19. How many countries use the Euro?
a. 27   b. 20   c. 16   d. 13

20. True or False: Egypt has the most pyramids in the world.

21. Which country has the longest official name, at 56 letters?

22. How many countries in South America do not border Brazil?
a. 2   b. 3   c. 4   d. 5

23. In which Asian country were early humans, the Homo floresiensis or 'hobbits', discovered?

24. In which country would you find the only rainforest in Europe?
a. Scotland   b. Bosnia and Herzegovina   c. Italy   d. Croatia

25. What is considered to be the most vegetarian country in the world?
a. Romania   b. India   c. Canada   d. Belgium

26. True or false: pilots and copilots never eat the same meal on flights.

27. In which country is riding a bicycle most popular, with 26% of all trips involving a bike?

ANSWERS

EUROPE

1. Italy
2. The Pyrenees mountains
3. c - 3690 km
4. a - Austria
5. d - 16
6. Estonia, Latvia, and Lithuania
7. d - Bratislava
8. b - 5,642 meters
9. d - Spain
10. Mont Blanc in France
11. The Italian and Balkan Peninsula
12. d - 32
13. c - Portugal
14. Guernsey, Alderney, and Sark
15. a - Poland
16. Emerald Isle
17. Paris
18. Spain and Portugal
19. c - The Pink City
20. d - Glasgow
21. b - Helsinki, Finland
22. c - 5
23. Vatican City
24. b - Switzerland
25. d - Norway
26. France
27. c - Lake Ladoga in Russia
28. La Sagrada Familia
29. Stone Henge
30. a - 44
31. The Tiber
32. d - Monaco
33. b - 7 million
34. The Vatican City
35. a - Iceland
36. c - Belarus
37. c - Aegean Sea
38. d - 8 Alpine countries
39. Geirangerfjord
40. c - Italy has the most sites
41. Great Britain
42. b - Valletta, Malta
43. The Acropolis
44. a - Portugal
45. Oslo
46. The Mediterranean Sea
47. The river begins in Germany and ends in Ukraine before draining out into the Black sea
48. San Marino and Vatican City
49. d - Spain
50. Ukraine
51. d - The Scandinavian Peninsula is the largest
52. Rotterdam in the Netherlands has the largest and busiest port
53. c - 4 countries
54. Budapest
55. Sweden
56. Sweden
57. c - 188,000
58. d - 2020
59. Rome, Italy
60. b & e - Austria & Slovakia

ASIA

1. Japan
2. b - The Yangtze River
3. b - 2760 km
4. China and India
5. China, and Pakistan
6. Mount Everest
7. a - The Tsushima Strait
8. Alaska
9. c - 36%
10. Gobi Desert
11. The Himalayas mountain range
12. d - Indonesia has the most islands with more than 17,500 islands
13. b - Cambodia
14. Manila
15. The Caspian Sea
16. a - Indonesia
17. Philippines
18. India and Bangladesh
19. Thailand
20. Karachi
21. c - Asia has 48 countries
22. c - Asia has 5 regions or subregions
23. d - China borders 14 countries
24. a - Mongolia
25. d - 12
26. Thailand
27. The Taj Mahal
28. b - 30%
29. False - It is growing at a rate of over 1cm per year
30. Tokyo-Yokohama, Japan (37.8 million people)
31. c - 4.7 billion people
32. South Korea
33. Komodo Islands
34. Ha Long Bay
35. Malè
36. Russia, Kazakhstan, Azerbaijan, Turkey, and Georgia are all possible answers
37. Malaysia, Indonesia, and Brunei
38. c - Rafflesia arnoldii
39. Hanoi
40. The Dead Sea

NORTH AMERICA

1. b - Mexico City
2. d - California
3. Missouri River & Mississippi River
4. Death Valley
5. Denali or Mount McKinley
6. Lake Superior
7. d - More than 700
8. b - Hispaniola
9. Mount Rushmore National Memorial
10. The Rio Grande
11. Canada is the largest
12. d - 23 countries
13. b - 54,000
14. The Rocky Mountains
15. Great Plains
16. b - 10
17. The Panama Canal
18. a - 86 metres
19. a - 57%
20. c - More than 80% of Greenland is covered in ice
21. Quebec
22. Ontario
23. d - Alaska
24. c - The Colorado River
25. b - The Cascade Range
26. Superior, Huron, Michigan, Erie, and Ontario
27. d - 20%
28. c - Nebraska
29. Mauna Loa
30. b - Toronto
31. Chihuahuan Desert and Mojave Desert
32. c - California

33. The Pacific Ocean, Atlantic Ocean, Arctic Ocean, and Gulf of Mexico
34. True
35. The Northern Lights
36. Ottawa
37. d - Wood Buffalo National Park
38. c - 6 timezones
39. Quebec
40. Golden Gate Bridge
41. Yellowstone National Park
42. b - Chihuahua
43. b - 31
44. The most common nickname is The Big Apple, but is also known as the City that Never Sleeps or Gotham among many others
45. a - The Pitons
46. The Bering Strait
47. c & d - Lake Erie and Lake Ontario
48. The Bridal Veil Falls
49. c - Colorado plateau
50. b - San Francisco
51. New York City
52. b - 4.5 million
53. d - New Mexico
54. b - 5.6 cm
55. Yukon River
56. Havana
57. a - The Tropic of Cancer
58. Greenland has an area of 2.166 million km² which is larger than the area of 1.973 million km² for Mexico
59. c - 4th
60. The word "America" comes from the name of Italian explorer Amerigo Vespucci

CENTRAL AMERICA

1. c - 7 countries make up Central America
2. b - Guatemala
3. a - Belmopan
4. Guatemala, El Salvador and Nicaragua
5. d - Belize
6. c - 28 national parks
7. a - 185 million
8. d - Belize
9. Panama
10. b - Guatemala
11. Lake Nicaragua
12. b - 3 million
13. a - Panama
14. United States Dollar
15. San José

SOUTH AMERICA

1. Salto Ángel (Angel Falls), Venezuela
2. The Andes
3. d & e - Bolivia and Paraguay
4. b - Northern Chile
5. d - Santa Cruz del Islote
6. d - 12 countries
7. b - Easter Island
8. Peru
9. Ecuador
10. b & c - Argentina and Chile
11. Buenos Aires
12. Colombia
13. c - 6992 km
14. The Inca Empire
15. c - Chile
16. The Atacama desert in Chile
17. Brazil
18. Aconcagua
19. Lake Titicaca
20. Brazil
21. d - São Paulo
22. Brazil
23. b - 60%
24. b - Coffee
25. Salar de Uyuni
26. c - 450 languages
27. The Galápagos Islands
28. Cape Horn
29. b - The Atacama Desert is 600 miles long
30. The Falkland Islands, French Guiana, and South Georgia and the South Sandwich Islands
31. La Paz at an elevation of 3,640 meters
32. b - Suriname
33. Brazil, Paraguay, Argentina, Chile, and Peru
34. c - 213 million
35. Colombia

AFRICA

1. Cape Town
2. South West Africa
3. b - 3333 km
4. Table Mountain
5. Mount Kilimanjaro
6. c - Asia
7. a - Algeria
8. c - Indian Ocean
9. South Africa
10. d - Uganda
11. d - 6650 km
12. b - Lake Victoria
13. d - Nigeria
14. The Sahara desert
15. Madagascar
16. Blyde River Canyon (Motlatse Canyon)
17. d - Mount Kenya
18. d - 54 countries
19. Egypt
20. Southern Rhodesia
21. c - The Horn of Africa
22. a - Seychelles, Saint Helena is smaller but it is a British overseas territory
23. The Dodo
24. d - Ouagadougou
25. Serengeti National Park
26. The mountains run from the Moroccan port of Agadir to the Tunisian capital of Tunis in the northeast
27. b - Kenya
28. c - Chad
29. c - 4,801,000
30. d - The Springbuck/springbok

AUSTRALASIA

1. a - Canberra
2. b - 169 islands
3. b - Queensland
4. c - Lake Te Anau
5. d - The Waikato River
6. Tonga
7. d - Papua New Guinea
8. b - Lake Eyre
9. New Zealand
10. Australia
11. Wellington
12. Ayers Rock or Uluru
13. Savaìi and Upolu
14. b - Rennell Island, one of the Soloman Islands
15. Christchurch
16. New South Wales
17. Papua New Guinea
18. d - New Zealand has around 600 islands
19. b - "land of the long white cloud"
20. Sydney, Australia
21. a - Hagåtña
22. b - Australia has 516 national parks
23. Milford Sound
24. Papua New Guinea
25. b - Nine islands

ANTARCTICA

1. c - 2,500 meters
2. b - Mount Vinson
3. The Atlantic, Pacific, and Indian Ocean
4. Yes, a recent study found 138 volcanoes in West Antarctica alone
5. Emperor penguins
6. d - Lambert Glacier
7. The Amundsen–Scott South Pole Station
8. c - Roald Amundsen
9. A desert
10. b - 7
11. a - Greenwich Mean Time
12. At the South Pole, where longitudes converge
13. a - The sun rises in late September and sets in late March
14. c - -89°C
15. c - 14 million km² (5.4 million square miles)

RIVERS AND LAKES

1. The Dead Sea
2. b - Colorado River
3. a - Murray River
4. The Amazon River
5. c - Great Britain
6. b - Fraser Island, Australia
7. Mekong river
8. Loch Ness
9. Headwaters
10. a - 1,642 m deep
11. a - Russia
12. a - Saudi Arabia
13. a - 61 m
14. Manitoulin Island
15. They are all saltwater lakes
16. Mackenzie River
17. c - France
18. c - 40 million people
19. The mouth
20. a - The River Severn
21. d - Utah, US
22. d - Finland
23. d - There are 117 million lakes on Earth
24. Limnologists
25. Martin Strel
26. b - The aquatic plant, Macarenia clavigera, on the riverbed causes the varied colours
27. A subterranean river is a river that runs beneath the ground's surface
28. c - The Philippines
29. b - 1200 km
30. Brazil

CAPITAL CITIES

1. Berlin
2. Turkey
3. Latvia
4. Bangkok, Thailand
5. Nairobi
6. Pyongyang
7. Wellington, New Zealand
8. b - Kingston
9. Paris
10. a - Lithuania
11. b - 11

12. Andorra, Djibouti, Guatemala, Kuwait, Luxembourg, Mexico, Monaco, Panama, San Marino, Singapore, Vatican City
13. d - Laos
14. Athens, Greece
15. b - Sierra Leone
16. b - Moscow, Russia
17. Sri Lanka
18. Jakarta
19. c - Nicaragua
20. Dublin, Ireland
21. Doha
22. Bangkok
23. South Korea
24. Zagreb
25. Barcelona, Spain
26. Tunisia
27. b - Phnom Penh
28. Beirut, Lebanon
29. d - Manila, Philippines
30. Quito

FLAGS

1. The maple leaf
2. d - Denmark
3. c - Six stars
4. The dragon
5. Ireland
6. b - 3
7. United Kingdom
8. Union Jack
9. a - Cyprus
10. b - Five stars
11. b - Red
12. c, d, e, f - Red, Yellow, Blue & Green
13. b - Circle
14. d - A crown
15. 'Il Tricolore'
16. a & f - Blue and white
17. d - Albania
18. Dragon
19. b - Sri Lanka
20. b - Lebanon
21. c - A snake
22. Vexillology
23. Indonesia
24. Vietnam
25. d - An AK-47
26. Nepal
27. Blue, white, and red
28. Star of David
29. a - 12
30. d - 26
31. Green, white and red
32. d - Oman
33. b - Somalia
34. b - Côte d'Ivoire
35. b & e - Red and white

GUESS THE COUNTRY

1. Germany
2. d - Iran
3. b - Thailand
4. Canada
5. d - Myanmar
6. d - Kenya
7. Jamaica
8. b - Colombia
9. Qatar
10. Ukraine
11. b - Afghanistan
12. Poland
13. Greece
14. a - Denmark
15. b - Japan
16. Malaysia
17. Morocco
18. c - Colombia
19. Cameroon
20. Sri Lanka
21. c - Czech Republic (czechia)
22. England
23. Lesotho
24. Iceland
25. Panama
26. c - Kuwait
27. Slovenia
28. Cyprus
29. Macau
30. Hungary

MOUNTAINS

1. The Alps
2. Brazil
3. France and Spain
4. d - Rocky Mountains
5. b - 10,210 m
6. c - 8,849 m
7. b - East coast
8. Lookout Mountain
9. Europe and Asia
10. USA, Canada, and France (Saint Pierre and Miquelon)
11. d - Bhutan
12. b - Tanzania
13. Ben Nevis
14. Everest, Aconcagua, Denali, Kilimanjaro, Mount Elbrus / Mont Blanc, Mount Vinson, Carstensz Pyramid / Mount Wilhelm / Mount Kosciuszko
15. a - 4,810 m
16. Alex Honnold
17. b - K2
18. c - Colorado
19. a - Japan
20. Annapurna
21. a - On average five people die each year
22. b - Wales
23. Canada
24. The Moon
25. Edmund Hillary and Tenzing Norgay
26. b - 1953
27. d - Germany
28. The Matterhorn
29. b - Mars, Olympus Mons has a height of over 21,900 m, and a diameter comparable to that of Arizona
30. Mount Cook

HISTORICAL GEOGRAPHY

1. Ceylon
2. b - 1935
3. a - 1939
4. Pangea
5. a - Zambia
6. Constantinople
7. The main reason for the change was to become a part of NATO, and also to distinguish itself from Greece
8. b - 2016
9. Bosnia and Herzegovina, Croatia, Macedonia, Montenegro, Serbia, and Slovenia
10. Eswatini
11. Pompeii
12. b - Burkina Faso
13. Petra
14. Ho Chi Minh City
15. The Moluccas
16. d - Cusco
17. The Great Wall of China
18. b - German South West Africa
19. a - Peking
20. c - Tanzania
21. b - Step Pyramid
22. a - Abyssinia
23. c - 1963
24. The Incas
25. United States, Great Britain, the Soviet Union, and France
26. b - 1994
27. d - 1989
28. b - Karakorum
29. d - Winchester
30. a - 1908

TOURISM

1. France (90m), Spain (83.7m), U.S (79.3m), China (65.7m), Italy (64.5m), Turkey (51.2m), Mexico (45m), Thailand (39.8m), Germany (39.6m), U.K (39.4m)
2. b - 9000
3. c - Thomas Cook
4. d - Less than 2 minutes. You can take this flight in Orkney, Scotland between the islands of Westray and Papa Westray
5. d - Japan
6. d - Germany and Spain
7. b - 62 million
8. c - 6: Heathrow, Gatwick, Stansted, London City, Luton & Southend
9. d - Argentina
10. c - Sticky rice
11. d - The Industrial Revolution
12. a - Iran
13. b - Japan
14. True
15. b - The Grand Tour
16. d - Great Smoky Mountains National Park
17. d - 33
18. a - 11%
19. c - 6 million+
20. b - Dominican Republic
21. Scotland
22. c - 5 - Monaco, Andorra, Liechtenstein, Vatican City and San Marino
23. True
24. c - The US
25. c - Beijing
26. d - The United States
27. b - Tuvalu
28. b - 1 in 5

29. a - Spain
30. False

NAME THE TOURIST ATTRACTION AND LOCATION

31. The Colosseum in Rome
32. The Sydney Opera House in Australia
33. The Louvre in Paris
34. The Sistine Chapel in The Vatican City
35. Macchu Picchu in Peru
36. Angkor Wat in Cambodia
37. Petra in Jordan
38. The Grand Canyon in the USA
39. Petronas Towers in Kuala Lumpur, Malaysia
40. Christ the Redeemer or Cristo Redentor in Brazil
41. The Leaning Tower of Pisa in Italy
42. The Burj Khalifa in Dubai
43. The Brandenburg Gate in Berlin
44. Central Park in New York
45. Bali in Indonesia
46. Stone Henge in England
47. Buckingham Palace in London
48. The French Quarter in New Orleans
49. Santorini in Greece
50. Salar de Uyuni, Bolivia

GUESS THE CITY

1. Istanbul, Turkey
2. Dubrovnik, Croatia
3. Munich, Germany
4. San Francisco, U.S
5. Manchester, UK
6. Geneva, Switzerland
7. Chicago, U.S
8. Las Vegas, U.S
9. Toronto, Canada
10. Timbuktu, Mali
11. Johannesburg in South Africa
12. Casablanca, Morocco
13. Lagos, Nigeria
14. Shanghai, China
15. Mumbai, India
16. Colombo, Sri Lanka
17. Ho Chi Minh City, Vietnam
18. Rio de Janeiro, Brazil
19. Perth, Australia
20. Auckland, New Zealand

LANGUAGES

1. a - Sanskrit
2. c - 43%
3. d - Papua New Guinea
4. a - Japanese (7.84 syllables per sec)
5. c - 4%
6. d - German
7. c - 6
8. Latin
9. d - Khmer in Cambodia, which has over 70 letters
10. b - Romanian
11. Dutch
12. a - Greek
13. d - Pinocchio
14. b - 44
15. b - Kinshasa, Democratic Republic of the Congo
16. Tagolog
17. c - Bolivia
18. Neuter
19. True
20. d - 20

POLITICAL GEOGRAPHY

1. c - 54
2. a - Australia, which became independent Jan 1st, 1901
3. a - Denmark
4. b - East Timor / Timor-Leste
5. India and Pakistan
6. c - Norway
7. b - France
8. c - 2 cents
9. The Scramble for Africa
10. a - The Canary Islands
11. d - Netherlands
12. Hong Kong
13. d - 15
14. c - 65
15. Sudan and South Sudan
16. Hawaii
17. c - Gibraltar
18. European Union
19. a - Cornwall
20. c - Texas

TERMINOLOGY

1. Fjord
2. a - Latitude
3. Canal
4. Suburb
5. Archipelago
6. b - Longitude
7. Lagoon
8. Geyser
9. d - Cartography
10. b - Antipodes
11. Strait
12. Altitude
13. Delta
14. Estuary
15. Primal Meridian
16. Savanna
17. Gulf
18. Equator
19. Enclave
20. Peninsula

NATURAL DISASTERS

1. Richter Scale
2. China
3. c - Morphian
4. Haiti
5. d - 9.5
6. b - Floods
7. False - Tornados usually only last up to an hour, whereas hurricanes can last up to three weeks, and tornadoes have much higher wind speeds
8. d - 525 m
9. c - Myanmar
10. b - 228,000
11. True
12. a - 70,000
13. Krakatoa
14. d - Colombia
15. Landslide
16. Crevasse
17. Pyroclastic flow
18. Great Galveston Storm (1900)
19. Avalanche
20. d - Florida
21. False - 85% of wildfires in the US are started by humans
22. c - China
23. c - Drought
24. b - Ring of Fire
25. d - 90%
26. Spanish flu
27. b - 14th
28. Plague of Justinian
29. Smallpox
30. Antonine Plague

CLIMATE CHANGE

1. b - Carbon dioxide
2. d - 99%
3. b - 0.8°C
4. b - 21 cm
5. Paris Agreement
6. c - 50%
7. c - Chlorofluorocarbons (CFCs)
8. b - Antarctica
9. d - There are over 5 trillion pieces of plastic in the ocean, as well as over 24 trillion pieces of microplastic
10. False - The number of tropical storms has increased significantly
11. Carbon sink
12. c - Cattle
13. c - 20%
14. True
15. b - 500
16. a - China
17. c, e & f - Japan, Norway and Iceland
18. d - 14%
19. d - 21.5 million people
20. d - 1,150 m

OCEANS AND SEAS

1. c - 71%
2. c - 96.5%
3. The Pacific Ocean
4. The Challenger Deep in the Mariana Trench
5. a - 10,935 m
6. d - Atlantic Ocean
7. The Southern Ocean
8. b - 3,700 m
9. b - Black Sea
10. The Mediterranean Sea
11. Arctic Ocean
12. Caspian Sea
13. Australia and New Zealand
14. Atlantic
15. Panama Canal
16. Iceland
17. c - 3
18. Indian Ocean
19. Pacific Ocean
20. Atlantic Ocean
21. c - 240,000
22. True
23. a - 7%
24. d - Triple the size
25. c - 3
26. The Atlantic Ocean
27. c - 65,000 km
28. a - 5%
29. d - At least 50%
30. False - There is about 500 times as much plastic in our oceans as stars in our galaxy

GEOLOGY

1. a - Diamond
2. Metamorphic
3. Igneous
4. Pyrites
5. Stalactite
6. b - Granite
7. Earthquakes
8. Sedimentary rock
9. b - Ammonites
10. Amber
11. d - Green
12. c - Spain
13. a - Corundum
14. Continental crust
15. Paleontology

ECONOMIC GEOGRAPHY

1. 1 - Luxembourg, 2 - Singapore, 3 - Ireland, 4 - Switzerland
2. b - 3.6%
3. d - 10 times
4. b - Luxembourg
5. US
6. b - $21 trillion
7. d - Japan
8. China
9. b - 13%
10. d - California
11. a - $2.15
12. b - 8%
13. c - 50%
14. a - $7.25
15. a - 8.2%
16. c - Argentina
17. c - Global Life & Health Insurance Carriers
18. a - £29,600
19. Purchasing power
20. b - 10%

ANAGRAM ROUND

10 ANAGRAMS OF COUNTRIES.

1. Germany
2. Tanzania
3. Australia
4. Indonesia
5. Mexico
6. Uzbekistan
7. South Africa
8. Algeria
9. Malaysia
10. Iceland

10 ANAGRAMS OF U.S STATES.

1. Connecticut
2. Indiana
3. Nebraska
4. Rhode Island
5. Wisconsin
6. Tennessee
7. Pennsylvania
8. North Dakota
9. New Mexico
10. Montana

10 ANAGRAMS OF CAPITAL CITIES.

1. Copenhagen
2. Warsaw
3. Bucharest
4. Ljubljana
5. Beijing
6. Singapore
7. Cairo
8. Wellington
9. Hanoi
10. Brasilia

POPULATION STATS

1. a - 10%
2. a - 10%
3. d - 82%
4. b - 19%
5. c - 23%
6. a - 3.3%
7. Turkish
8. Scotland
9. c - 22%
10. d - 49%

GENERAL KNOWLEDGE

1. c - 14,000
2. Japan
3. True
4. True, the ban was introduced in 1994 to prevent the spread of disease to seals.
5. True - Their calendar is between 7-8 years behind ours.
6. b - Cost Rica
7. Iceland
8. United States
9. d - France
10. c - 1 in 3
11. False, it is the other way which is worse
12. a - 12,000, it would take around 27 years to visit a new one every day!
13. c - Hamburg
14. b - Portugal

15. California
16. Africa
17. c - The Philippines, which was named after King Philip II of Spain
18. b - 7, Kazakhstan, Tajikistan, Uzbekistan, Kyrgyzstan, Turkmenistan, Afghanistan, and Pakistan
19. b - 20
20. False, Sudan has the most pyramids
21. The United Kingdom of Great Britain and Northern Ireland
22. a - 2, Ecuador and Chile
23. Indonesia, on the island of Flores
24. b - Bosnia and Herzegovina
25. b - India
26. True
27. The Netherlands

Made in the USA
Columbia, SC
20 December 2024